Hurry, Spring!

Books by Sterling North
for readers of all ages

So Dear to My Heart
Abe Lincoln, Log Cabin to White House
George Washington
Young Thomas Edison
Thoreau of Walden Pond
Captured by the Mohawks
Mark Twain and the River
First Steamboat on the Mississippi
Rascal

Hurry, Spring!

By STERLING NORTH

Drawings by Carl Burger

E. P. DUTTON & CO., INC., NEW YORK

Published simultaneously in Canada by Clarke,
Irwin & Company Limited, Toronto and Vancouver

Library of Congress Catalog Card Number: 66–11387

First Edition

Designed by Hilda Scott

Lithographed by The Murray Printing Company

For Gladys

The girl for whom I built the cabin.

EARLY in March, even before all the snow has melted, Spring begins to ask questions.

In protected angles of the low stone walls the bulbs probe upward with green fingers to test the temperature. The striped chipmunk, the woodchuck, the bear and the raccoon peer from their winter dens to sniff the wind.

And from high above comes the clamorous questioning of great flocks of wild geese—true heralds of the spring— a sound filled with such hope and promise it might awaken the dead. Notice how often these wedges of geese are numbered in multiples of six! It is thought that they are then made up of whole families: a gander and goose, mated for life, and their year-old goslings.

When you see a single goose flying alone, it usually means that some hunter has killed its mate, and the widowed male or female is crying and searching for the family it no longer has. Sometimes a lone gander leads the flock into the wind, cutting the air for those behind him. The skein of geese "V's" out, like a well-proportioned jet, to take advantage of reduced air resistance.

A widowed gander often watches over the flock by night. While the other geese sleep with their heads beneath their wings, he remains awake and alert to warn of danger. The loyalty he gave his mate he now gives to the flock.

Tomorrow he may fly again at the apex of the wedge, leading the way, over mysterious pathways through the sky, toward the distant arctic nesting ground.

CAN you keep a thousand secrets? Spring can!

These secrets are within the seed, within the bud, within the mother and within the nest.

No seed ever forgets what variety it is. A rose is a rose, and never a geranium. Given rain and sunshine, the seed will break from its casing and struggle up through the earth to produce the violet or anemone in the grass; or, in a few hundred years, an enormous redwood tree.

Ever since the mating season during the previous autumn, the does have had secrets within them. So have the mother animals of many other species. They are all awaiting spring, to bring forth their young.

[2]

Most of the birds have started northward, but have not completed their journey. How do they find their way for thousands of unmarked miles through storms and darkness? That is their secret.

If you watch and listen closely, Spring will teach you many of its secrets. For you, too, are one of Spring's precious secrets.

THE Indians called March the "Maple Moon."

They liked maple sugar as much as you do. Indians disliked salt, calling it "bitter," and instead used maple sugar to season meat, wild rice, Indian corn meal and almost everything else they ate, including fish.

When the snow began to melt in late February or early March, they moved from their winter villages into the maple forests to tap the trees and boil down the sweet sap. A good housewife had many birchbark buckets to hang beneath the spigots on her trees, and she had hereditary rights to her part of the maple grove. If very lucky, she also had a huge brass kettle that was much better than earthenware pots for making syrup and sugar.

Indians, as well as white settlers, danced and sang during March when the sap was running. They tossed syrup into the snow to make maple candy. They were so happy that sometimes even the braves (who scorned most labor as "squaw's work") would carry a few buckets of sap or bring wood to keep the fires burning under the kettles. They also carved wooden molds representing various birds and animals. In these molds they cast maple sugar to offer as gifts to those they loved.

Every spring we should celebrate the Maple Moon.

BEFORE spring becomes fragrant, it becomes slightly less than fragrant.

If you really love skunks and skunk cabbages—which are not even remotely related—you will think of their somewhat similar odor as pungent, even refreshing (but in small doses).

Skunks wander many miles early in the spring, hunting for mates. Later in the spring the little ones are born —as charming as the name "woods kittens" would suggest. The marking varies from nearly pure black, with only a white star on the head, to narrow-striped and broad-striped patterns. These kittens follow their mother Indian file. A mother and four babies walking in the moonlight once went right down the path that happened to run through the middle of a pup tent where a canoeing friend and I were trying to sleep. If not disturbed, they never spray their defensive tear gas. Fed on bread and milk and kept away from bad dogs and bad boys, they make charming pets.

The skunk cabbage, which is frequently the first flower one sees each spring, is a first cousin to the calla lily and the Jack-in-the-pulpit. This admirable and slightly odoriferous plant grows in moist places and sends up its large cone-shaped spathes of mottled purple through ground that is usually still partly frozen.

Skunks eat almost everything, including insects, berries and mice. But I have never seen a skunk eat skunk cabbage. It may be a case of honor among perfumers.

MORE sunshine, more color!

Broken by the prism of water or glass, sunshine shatters into the rainbow.

The equatorial jungle produces more colorful birds. Tropical countries produce more color in human dress and human habitations. Painters who have visited the tropics often go wild with color in their paintings.

Spring, moving northward, brings color back to the landscape. Usually by the 15th of March the red-winged blackbirds and the wood ducks have returned to our little lake above the waterfall in our enchanted valley near Morristown, New Jersey. They will stay all summer, and nest here.

The scarlet epaulet on the redwing is perhaps the brightest decoration ever placed upon the shoulder of a liquid songster, swaying in ecstasy upon a cattail or a willow withe.

The wood duck is the most beautiful bird in North America. The gaudy drake's modest mate is as quietly brown as the female mallard, but with a white eye streak that makes her look perpetually startled. The bold male has a proud crest, ruby, emerald and purple feathers and bright yellow legs. His breast, or "gorget," is an entire sunset.

Later this pair will have eight to twelve puffballs in

their nest in a hollow beech. These ducklings will move as swiftly as their parents, tumble over the waterfall without harm, and evade almost any predator except the snapping turtle, who with reptilian stealth pulls these charming bits of thistledown to their deaths.

We shoot no living thing on these twenty-seven acres except snapping turtles. And this because we love wood ducklings and have raised a few for the pleasure they give us, walking the piano keys, and peering from the picture windows.

Even Thoreau and Audubon failed to do justice to these beautiful birds. Thoreau called them, oddly, "Summer Ducks." And Audubon, great bird painter though he was, totally missed their brilliance in his Elephant Folio. Spring *must* be here. In our little lake the wood ducks are flashing signals to the sun itself across the sparkling water.

IF you try to argue with Spring, it argues right back.

Dump a layer of snow six inches thick all over its new greenery and it shakes it off, melts it off, laughs it off and comes up smiling.

The cardinals never for one moment believe that winter has really returned. So they continue to whistle, "What cheer."

Far above the valley, riding an updraft of warm air, a hawk circles without stirring a wing. He owns the world from horizon to horizon.

HE was known as "Willow Pete" and he lived in a hut he had built among the willows, and made his living from them. He was almost as much the spirit of spring as the red-winged blackbird swaying and singing on a willow wand.

All of the children of my native town in Wisconsin were told to stay away from Willow Pete. He was a bad influence. Sometimes he was rather eccentric. But he loved children, and they loved him. He told them stories that thrilled them, entranced them and sometimes gave them nightmares, as he wove his willow baskets.

With the first breath of spring the willows put forth brave pussies, gray and soft and pleasant to the touch. This was the sign to Willow Pete that his willow sprouts were pliant and ready for weaving into baskets of every size and shape. There was scarcely a housewife in town whose clothesbasket or market basket had not been woven by Pete, who charged fifty cents for the small ones and a dollar for the very large ones. No two were exactly alike because they were not simple basket weave, but displayed all manner of fanciful designs to please the whims of the basket weaver.

A harmless old man, a gentle old man, he lived and wove, and told his stories among the willows. And there, in time, he died and was buried. The redwings sang his requiem.

DAY and Night have a vigorous tug of war that goes on all year.

Throughout the cold months, the nights have been longer than the days. But as spring approaches, Night knows it is losing this contest.

On the first moment of real spring, around March 21st, the vernal equinox gives us twenty-four hours in which

Night and Day are evenly matched (each of twelve hours' duration).

The very word "equinox" means "equal night."

Very slowly and stubbornly, Night gives way to Day throughout the spring. More sunshine means more grass, more flowers, more little animals being brought into a warmer, kinder world.

"I'm winning," says the Sunshine.

"We're losing gracefully," say the Moonlight and the Starlight.

And so it goes, right up to the last day of spring, which is about June 22nd and is called the "summer solstice," when the days are the longest of the year.

But night will again have its turn, for each night after June 22nd becomes a little longer until, on the autumnal equinox, once again Day and Night are evenly matched.

And the great Moon says to the Stars, "I knew we could do it. It happens every year."

SPRING is a song, and each of us can sing it.

Spring is a dance, and each of us can dance it.

Spring is the feeling that we can fly like the birds, glide like the flying squirrels, scoot down slippery mud slides into the water, like the playful otters.

The new sunshine lures the mallards to follow each other—one male and one female—in nuptial flights. They preen, dip (bottoms up), lift their wings, rise from the shining water for acrobatic flights through the air. Usually the modest brown female leads the flamboyant emerald-headed drake in the wild flight through the sky above the lake. Almost as though they could sense

by radar the slightest change of direction, they dart, veer, rise into the clouds and glide down to the lake again. Perhaps they choose each other by how well they fly together. In time they mate and have a nest filled with as many as twelve or fifteen eggs. The mother protects and leads her floating ducklings when they hatch.

Many other birds go through characteristic courting dances. The ruffed grouse and related birds drum, strut, or puff out their air sacks, displaying vivid colors and entrancing rhythms. The flickers weave back and forth on either side of a fence post.

> Hide-and-seek.
> Back and forth.
> You go that way.
> I'll go this way.

And perhaps nothing is more amusing than the blue jays who have been screaming at each other all year, snatching every bite from a mate all winter.

The male blue jay acts like a teen-age boy inviting his girl friend to a dance or a drive-in. He says:

"Look, darling, here is the best little white grub I have found in weeks. Why don't you eat it?" And he cuddles up to the girl he has been beating up all winter.

"Are you kidding?" asks the young female blue jay. "Well, just for you."

Next week they will both be busy finding strong rootlets, tugging, pulling and sometimes falling over backward on their blue-and-white tails. They weave these rootlets into a nest where they can hatch their eggs and have another batch of difficult blue jays who won't feel loving for at least a year.

ONE spring we were sure we saw the tracks of a small bear in the melting snow and later in the sand along the edge of the lake. This seemed un- likely, since there have been very few bears in New Jersey in the last half century. However, nothing but a bear could have come down so flat-footed, saying with all four paws, "I really am a fine little bear."

Frightened neighbors reported it to the police and to the local papers:

"Help, help, a bear!"

We thought it was the bear, and not the neighbors who needed help.

Unfortunately, in the six months he was in our valley we never saw him. There were a few trees where he left his mark as high as a little bear could scratch. One night his paw prints were on our back porch where we feed raccoons, possums, foxes and skunks. Apparently he had fished a few big trout out of the stream and had enjoyed a feast of honey from our bee tree. He also liked our berries. But he had done no serious damage.

Came autumn, and the season when our local murderers shoot even the pet deer clearly marked with ribbons around their necks. Out came the brave hunters, and one spotted our little bear, perhaps the only bear in New Jersey.

This Daniel Boone shot in "self-defense," and is still bragging about the fact that he killed the last bear in Harding Township.

WHEN there is an oversupply of the little rodents called lemmings, they seem to be bright enough to march to the sea and reduce their numbers.

But every spring most of the birds and animals of the world forget that there are sometimes too many of their species. The fish in the rivers and the sea lay millions of eggs to try to produce more fish of their kind. The birds struggle northward despite wind and storm and dangerous insecticides. They find mates, build nests, lay eggs and have one or more families of nestlings.

The does have fawns, often twins if the soil of their forest is fertile. The raccoon mothers have from two to seven babies. The wild ducks lay from ten to fifteen eggs, brood upon them and hatch a whole flotilla of ducklings.

Spring always says, "Despite all the animals that might destroy our eggs or our babies, despite murderous mankind, the greatest predator on earth, we will have offspring, we will protect and train them, we will bring them to maturity if we can." Long live the raccoons, deer and wood ducks. Long live all our gentle forest neighbors!

DO the glossy black crows and ravens shout "Nevermore"? Or do they shout "Evermore"?

After many years of watching crows, and owning a few, we would definitely vote for "Evermore."

They are the very substance of lusty life and curiosity and courage. They never take "no" for an answer, and will perch on the shoulders of a scarecrow, stay out of range of any shotgun, steal corn if they wish, and otherwise proclaim that field and forest are their own. They hold town meetings of the air as they flap along in a posse, chasing a hawk or a fox or a stray cat.

The crow, like the jay and the magpie (who are his mischievous cousins), will brag or lie or steal a bright object without the least sense of guilt. But they never try to hide their true character, and they will fight anything from a raccoon to a vulture.

For several seasons some thirty turkey vultures and as many raucous crows have battled for a huge dead oak tree on the granite ridge above our house. The vultures, with a wingspread of at least six feet, far greater than that of any crow, have valiantly tried to capture the rookery.

Who always wins? The crows of course!

And long after we are gone, the brave and noisy crows and ravens still will be crying:

"Evermore!"

Blue jays and crows,
Blue jays and crows!
Now what's the rumpus?
Heaven only knows!

"Let's buzz-bomb a fox.
Let's harry a hawk.
Let's scream at a cat
Who is taking a walk."

In blue cutaway
The immaculate jay
Cries, "What do you say?
Boys, what do you say?"

"A crow's never craven,"
Caws Poe the pet raven;
"So, on to the fray!
Let's make it a day."

"I'll give them some shocks,"
Sulks Reynard the Fox;
"I'll catch me a jay
Or a crow, someday!"

ALL through our woods, where the surrounding hills rise like a green amphitheater above the clear little lake, our orchestra is tuning up for spring. The wood winds, horns, strings and the percussion section are trying their instruments and running their scales.

A mockingbird seems to think he is the conductor. He can play all the instruments and sing all the songs. He leaps into the air from the tall stump of a dead tree, flashing black-and-white signals to his orchestra— crescendo, diminuendo— Up, up, wood winds; a little quiet there on the drums.

The wood winds play most of the solos this afternoon. They are the thrushes who produce pure and flutelike music. Wood thrush, hermit thrush, bluebird and robin —liquid and lovely. They take their cue from the stream that flows over several small waterfalls into the lake. Who would think that a robin has fifty-two notes? Or that the rose-breasted grosbeak (not a thrush) can outsing the robin?

Until the peepers come forth with their highest strings, or the bullfrogs with their lowest bass fiddles, it is perhaps the cello of the mourning dove that gives the valley its mood.

Night will come soon with another sort of symphony—almost as silent as the wings of a great horned owl or the footfall of a fox, the music of the distant planets and stars, the harmony of the great universe as the spring night enfolds us.

IT is often said that an Englishman's home is his castle. The nest of a bird and the surrounding territory are equally well defended.

Song sparrows, like so many other birds, post "no trespassing" signs at the four corners of their private estates. But what delightful warnings, consisting solely of bird song. "Mine, mine, mine," warbles the male bird protecting his territory. "Wife and chi, chi, chi, chi, children."

The male song sparrows arrive at least as early as the robins and the red-winged blackbirds in our valley. The females come later. And one pair always nests in the same protected spot above a stone wall in a thicket of Dorothy Perkins roses. The male immediately stakes out a feeding territory approximately one hundred by one hundred feet. He sings his surveyed limits from a white lilac to the west, a sumac to the south and a red dogwood to the east, while our house itself protects his northern border.

He sings 18 times every 5 minutes, and I have counted 1,862 songs in a single day. You would think that his little throat would be quite raw after such a day-long concert. But next day at dawn he is up and at it again. When needful, he bluffs or fights other song sparrows, and sometimes birds of other species twice his size who dare invade his little kingdom. He even fights his own mirror image in the window, as do robins. "Looks too much like me. Guess I'll have to fight," he says as he views himself in this mirror.

Most of us hear only five or six variations to his song, but careful recordings show that his species has a "language" of over eight hundred musical phrases.

There is a *V* for Victory on the breast of the song sparrow.

SOME of the song sparrows stay all winter. Other hardy sparrows, particularly the handsome white-throats, the lusty and ruddy fox sparrows, the tree sparrows and the rowdy Falstaffian English sparrows (actually weaver finches), brave the snow and freezing blasts to feed with the cardinals, cheerful chickadees, titmice, downy woodpeckers and nuthatches all through the coldest months.

We once had a neighbor so stupid that she called all

sparrows, and all other little brown birds, "spigs."

"Mess up my eaves," said this embittered widow woman, "so I got my Jimmy an air rifle to shoot them spigs."

Jimmy managed to kill a great many sparrows, thrushes, wrens and other "spigs," whereupon his enlightened mother turned him loose on a new menace, the "darning needles." As she explained, "They'll sew your mouth shut."

"Darning needles" turned out to be gossamer dragonflies, ruby-throated hummingbirds and sphinx moths, which at dusk look a little like the hummingbird—all utterly harmless, and charming in their amazing ability to hover on thin air.

"Shoot 'em dead, Jimmy. They'll sew your mouth shut."

LET us suppose that it is spring, but 125 years ago. You are a young man in love with a beautiful Swedish girl who is "below your social level." You are the most brilliant student of birdlore who has ever graduated from the great University of Uppsala.

You ask your parents and your King, "May I please marry this lovely girl, although she is a commoner?"

Your parents say *no* and the King says *no*. What do you do? If you stay in Sweden, and reject her, you will be the Royal Ornithologist. If you decide to marry her, the King and your aristocratic parents will disown you.

Thure Ludwig Theodor Kumlien (1819–1888) hesitated only a few days. Soon after, he sailed with his sweetheart for North America and southern Wisconsin, and staked out a hard-earned claim to eighty acres adjoining the big farm owned by my grandfather. As a small boy, my father collected birds' eggs and abandoned nests for Kumlien, and lived ninety-nine years to tell the story. Only one egg was taken from a nest, and the mother bird always supplied the lack. The priceless collections of eggs went to at least a dozen museums. Kumlien corresponded in many languages with scientists all over the world. The Kumlien gull, aster and anemone were named for this great Wisconsin naturalist.

In 1918, in the virgin forest that Kumlien had preserved, I listened to my first pair of whippoorwills as the full moon rose over the lake. And I decided at that moment that I would spend the rest of my life heeding the voices of the birds and animals. I hope that those who read this book will realize that every returning spring means more to me because of a romantic ornithologist named Kumlien.

MANY of us think that spring has not fully arrived until we hear the first peeper hitting some note above high *C:* "Peep-peep-peep-peep." Like so many other amphibians, this little brown creature, with a cross on his back and bars on his legs, has spent the winter deep in the marsh. But now that the afternoon temperature reaches fifty degrees, he feels a sudden urge to arise and sing.

Up he comes to the edge of the lake, eager to join the birds in the spring chorus.

"Well, here you are," say the redwings.

"Yes, here I am," says the peeper. "Peep-peep. Right in tune with spring."

PROBABLY the most modest and most delicate of all the spring bulbs is the scilla, or pretty blue squill. Its six-petaled flowers scattered along our walking and riding trails form blue pools, often at the base of big beech trees, looking so much like sky water that you expect the mirror image of a cloud to pass across the surface.

There are at least fifteen references to lilies in the Bible, most of them lyrical, but not all (scientifically) lilies. But if we "consider the lilies of the field" and include the scilla, it is easy to see why they "toil not, neither do they spin." Any flower of this ethereal blue enjoys a life-long pension on our estate.

IT is very hard to wait for spring. When my wife and I were children, we thought the time would never come for playing marbles, spinning tops, jumping ropes, climbing trees, wading in puddles, roller-skating or going fishing. Hurry, Spring!

When we were fifteen, and first in love, it was hard to

wait until I could launch my canoe and take Gladys across our gleaming Wisconsin lake.

Now we are nearly 60, but we are still impatient for spring. So almost every year we meet spring halfway, in North Carolina or Virginia or at least at Cape May, which is the southernmost tip of New Jersey, where most migrating birds of the eastern flyway cross Delaware Bay. We live in New Jersey, so the Cape is only a pleasant drive down the Garden State Parkway to the shining beaches strewn with bright shells and rounded quartz pebbles called "Cape May diamonds."

It wasn't the "diamonds" that brought the fierce pirate Captain Kidd to Cape May. It was the Lily Pond almost at the point of the Cape, which, although barely above sea level, is a fresh-water, spring-fed pond. Whalers, men-of-war, pirate ships and all manner of craft have used this pond for nearly three centuries to fill their water casks. And there it is today, not far from the 170-foot lighthouse, with its magnificent quarter-million-candle-power lamp that throws its beam for nineteen miles.

Another pond not much farther inland is alive and afloat with more water birds than we have ever seen elsewhere in our lives: Canada geese, snow geese, blue geese, whistling swans, mute swans, a black swan that must have been imported from Australia, blue- and green-winged teal, the little ruddy duck that can go downwind a mile a minute, glowing like an ember; canvasback, black ducks, mallards and wood ducks, and the very rare cattle egret. The male mute swan was the majestic emperor of this entire pond, having a ferocious temper and great pride because his wife was on her nest. He carried his wings cocked at a jaunty angle, and decided that the pieces of doughnuts we were tossing to all the birds rightly belonged exclusively to him.

After visiting this second pond, we wandered down a country road abloom with gardens grown wild, white with a surf of beach plums, and lavender with oxalis, a tiny flower that on close examination looks a little like the wild geranium. We came across three black lambs in a pasture painted with spring flowers.

For half an hour we listened to the serenade of a mockingbird. These birds are clowns, mimics, virtuosos, and full of vitality, running through countless imitations of other bird songs, and well aware of the fact they have an audience. This character ran back and forth along the ridgepole of an old deserted building among blooming lilacs. He looked into the broken windows, peered under the eaves and leaped skyward with each burst of radiant song.

After a few days of surf fishing and shell hunting, we followed the bird migration up the state to our own valley where many of the flowers had now come into bloom.

THE robin, like the bluebird, is a thrush, and he sings like a thrush. But because his brick-red waistcoat is so commonly known and his "Cheer, cheer, cheer" so frequently heard, he is discounted and unjustly taken for granted.

Actually, the robin is a most admirable bird. He is likely to be the first to sing in the morning, and the last to speak a quiet evensong as darkness descends. He is ever cheerful in fog or rain or late frost, nearly the first to come in the spring and the last to leave in the fall. Sometimes he stays all winter, and, like the cardinal, blooms amid the snowdrifts.

In the spring he leads a chorus of birds, some in no way related, but possibly influenced by his songs. The scarlet tanager joins the robin choral society, singing like a robin with bronchitis. The rose-breasted grosbeak from a top twig is a glorified robin who has had a few singing lessons.

Robins of both sexes make devoted mates and fledgling feeders. What would spring be without the robin?

SPRING is a *Rhapsody in Blue*—blue sky and water, blue scilla along the blue-stoned woodland paths, robin's-egg blue in the nests beneath the eaves.

But only a few of our favorite birds wear blue—the great blue heron wading stealthily among the shallows at the edge of the lake, stalking little frogs and minnows; the loud and violent kingfisher, screaming at every intruder and diving from high in the air for aquatic delicacies; the blue jay, who becomes a fond lover when the mating season arrives, but is almost ashamed to let the world know that he has a "whisper song" for his mate or that he feeds her tenderly while she is on the nest.

It is seldom the biggest birds who have the most beautiful songs. The real rhapsody comes from the throats of the bluebirds and the indigo buntings.

The bluebird is one of the gentlest of all our spring arrivals, carrying "the sky on his back," as Henry Thoreau expressed it. The breast of both male and female is roseate in hue. If you have a suitable hollow tree or fence post or a birdhouse with an entrance measuring one and one-half inches in diameter, a pair of bluebirds may honor you with a visit lasting most of the summer.

The mother bluebird usually lays four to six pale-blue eggs, and in about twelve days these eggs hatch into enormously hungry fledgelings that the father feeds and later trains to nourish themselves while their mother refurbishes the nest or builds a new one for a second brood.

While other members of the thrush family, particularly the hermit thrush, are more accomplished singers, the bluebirds warble several liquid notes. And, like the cardinal, they are a rare species in which the female, as well as the male, sings charmingly. Some interpret the song as saying "Ber-muda, Ber-muda."

The even more vivid indigo bunting averages in length some five and one-half inches, which is an inch and a half shorter than the bluebird. His song is also soft and tender and modest—"Sweet, sweet, sweet, swit, swit, sway—sway-sway-sway-sway, sweet sweet."

It takes all the songs of all of the blue-tinted birds to compose Spring's *Rhapsody in Blue.*

"APRIL is the cruelest month," as the poet T. S. Eliot has thoughtfully observed. It was the cruelest month for me when, at the age of seven, I saw my mother surrounded with April hyacinths, white as the satin that lined her coffin.

She looked as though she were merely sleeping. The lines of worry and care had somehow left her face. Her eyelids were closed, and her skin seemed as smooth as it must have been when she graduated from college at the age of eighteen, valedictorian of her class, adept in botany, history and several languages.

She had taught the older children almost everything they knew; had helped them to become poets able to take the *St. Nicholas* Gold Medal. Only a few days before her death she had decided that a poem I had just written was good enough to be sent to *St. Nicholas*, but she did not live to see it published.

Below the windows there was a small garden of wild flowers she had helped me find and transplant—several varieties of violets, anemones, bluebells, wild geraniums and the pink wild roses of Wisconsin. She could not smell them now; she could not even smell the almost overwhelming fragrance of the hyacinths.

That was more than fifty years ago, and only this April have I had the courage to raise hyacinths again. It took half a century for me to bear the perfume of that flower.

WHEN I was a boy in Wisconsin, spring always meant trolling for pike and pickerel on wide Lake Koshkonong from a boat usually rowed by my father, or casting wet flies or bass plugs into the deep, dark pool below the dam in Rock River at Indian Ford.

Every sandbar had its willow grove, alive with red-winged blackbirds. Jacksnipe zigzagged over, so swift and evasive that few hunters could murder them. The kill-deer flashed ahead of the storm, piping "Killdee, killdee" to warn of the coming wind and rain. Spring was the season for launching my canoe and daring the whitecaps, the swift currents and the rapids. The midwestern mead-owlarks, so much more melodious than the eastern meadowlarks, made the valleys echo with song.

I was very young, and despite the loss of my mother, I could fish and swim and canoe, and I was in love (first, last and always) with Gladys.

The great fish of that era struck the lure and were slowly brought to net. The streams and rivers ran full and clean. The wild ducks and geese and a few swans came northward up the great Mississippi flyway. And some of my poems were being published in eastern maga-zines. In the hours when I could forget my sadness, it was a good time to be alive.

BIRDS' nests are among the most fascinat-ing phenomena of the natural world. Various birds use horsehair, snakeskins, feathers, fur and down, pebbles or shells, moss, mud and leaves to build predictable homes. Yearlings, with no chance of training in the art, but perhaps with a memory of the nest in which they were reared, invariably build nests just like those built by their mothers and fathers and ancestors for countless generations.

The ruby-throated hummingbird builds a nest of green lichens and cobwebs smaller than a silver dollar, with eggs the size of your little fingernail. The nests look so much like a knot on the upper side of a branch that I have positively identified only two in my life, although

we have hummingbirds probing our flowers each season.

The first hummingbird nest I ever saw was discovered under rather dramatic circumstances. In the year 1922, when I was fifteen and my father nearly sixty, I worked all summer on a two-hundred-acre-farm, clearing virgin soil, cultivating corn and tobacco, and laboring fourteen hours a day, thirteen and a half days every fortnight. My pay was $25 a month. During that August I fell unconscious in the field, stricken with polio. In my delirium I talked about a hummingbird's nest in a white oak tree in the middle of the south field. And my father went to the farm, climbed the tree, and examined all the limbs and brought back the abandoned hummingbird's nest to help his son regain his consciousness and eventual health.

Now I am near the age my father was at that time, and there is just such a delicate nest of cobwebs and lichens in a tree beyond our window. I could not climb that tree even for a hummingbird's nest. Doubtless I will never reach my father's great age. But I have inherited an undeserved legacy. Agassiz called Kumlien the greatest expert on bird nests in the world. My father learned much from Kumlien on this subject, and I learned a little from my father. At least I know the nest of a hummingbird, song sparrow, robin, ovenbird, hawk, mallard or osprey when I see one. And I step very carefully through the meadows, particularly when I see a meadowlark or killdeer with a drooping wing, pitifully pretending she is wounded as she leads us away from her nest among the grass and pebbles.

SOME forty-odd years ago this spring, when the forest trees were barely misted over with new green, I started building a cabin of limestone and hewn oak on the banks of Rock River not far from my boyhood town of Edgerton, Wisconsin. Many of the slabs of limestone that I quarried from the steep bank into which I was building the cabin weighed several hundred pounds. Some of the eighteen-foot hewn-oak logs weighed more than half a ton. Since I was not long off crutches, following a siege of infantile paralysis, it sometimes took many hours with rollers and levers to get a block of stone or a log into place. But I would not let anyone help me, since this was to be the home of my high-school sweetheart and myself.

The beautifully hewn logs were already seventy-five years old, and came from a barn where they had been seasoned until they were as hard as iron. It took frequent sharpening of the one-man crosscut saw, as I fashioned the neat joints at the corners of the cabin. Even so, the saw was often too hot to touch after its laborious journey through those oak twelve-by-twelves.

It was not a large cabin, but somewhat larger than Thoreau's on Walden Pond. Thirty feet above the water, on a 45-degree limestone bluff, it had a length of 18 feet and a width of 14. The larger room, which was 12 by 14, was literally quarried from the upper slope, with a fireplace at the rear that went up through native rock. The room in front of it, facing the river, was 6 by 14, and constituted a porch that was to be glassed in for winter use and screened for a summer terrace. But the steep bank made it necessary to build a heavy limestone foundation 7 feet high under this flightlike projection among the treetops. One hundred yards downriver, the water poured endlessly and musically over a wide dam into a pool 17 feet deep, and alive with fish.

Not all of my time could be spent on this delightful project, since this was my senior year of high school, and besides, I had to sell enough of my poetry to cover the cost of hinges and spikes, doors and windows, mortar and sand, pine rafters and roof boards. I had decided that only the rare dollars earned by writing serious lyric poetry was money appropriate for building a cabin for my love.

All too infrequently did her family allow her to come and watch me work. But those spring days were memorable as she sat in her blue cotton dress and sandals on a slab of limestone there above a river as blue as her dress.

My stepmother had told me I might build the cabin on her land. Then, as I finished it, after two summers of work, she changed her mind. In time teen-agers of quite another sort broke the windows, mutilated the walls, and finally tore it down completely.

Gladys and I now live in New Jersey in another—but

spacious—house that we designed, beside another dam and stream. But sometimes we go back to Wisconsin and sit for a while on the foundation of the old cabin we desired so deeply when we were seniors in high school.

IF you wish to hear a moonlight sonata as tender as that composed by Beethoven, listen to the English nightingale some moonlit night. It has inspired more poets than any bird except the skylark.

As Juliet said pleadingly to Romeo, trying to convince him it was far from dawn:

"It was the nightingale, and not the lark,
That pierc'd the fearful hollow of thine ear; . . ."

In America, alas, we have few nightingales save those confined in cages. But we do have a close competitor, the mockingbird; and a less-talented midnight contender, the whippoorwill.

Apparently here, in Morristown, New Jersey, we are near the northern limit of the mockingbird's warm-weather habitat. We have heard and seen only four or five in the last twenty-two years. But to drink our fill of their moonlight serenade we often go to the Williamsburg Inn in the Colonial capital of Virginia and take a favorite room overlooking the golf course and gardens.

[38]

The playful mimics who have been singing all day for the visitors, and putting on mock battles among the magnolias, wake again when the moon comes up to give us their purest and most varied melodies. We have counted as many as thirty-four completely dissimilar trills, runs and arpeggios, each following the last with scarcely a moment to compose the next number. They seem to be singing for joy, but also perhaps in competition with the other mockingbirds who, by daylight, danced and bluffed in territorial defiance, while also courting a handsome mate.

Almost unvaried come the pure voices of the whippoorwills answering one another. Their note is three clear and strongly emphasized syllables, thrice repeated: "Whip-poor-will, whip-poor-will, whip-poor-will." We have counted a repetition of this call 937 times on a single moonlit night.

Those who insist on sleeping miss a great deal of romance in this world.

SPRING comes northward at about fifteen miles a day, repeating this predictable miracle year after year. It starts in February in southern Florida (where seasons overlap), and advances with its green banners and winged scouts and outriders all the way to the arctic. It climbs mountains slowly, rushes up long valleys and takes by storm the laurel "thicks" and fruit orchards. If you want your dogwoods to stay in perfect bloom from February to June, you must follow the spring northward as did Edwin Way Teale.

Raccoons, like most other animals, know the perfect time to mate. They anticipate full spring by about sixty-three days, and thus have their two to seven kits when the season can best befriend them. In our valley the birthday of most of our little masked bandits is late April or early May.

In hollow maples, sycamores and other good "den trees" the mother raccoon gives birth to the softly furred and blind little creatures that for about two months will not leave the den. Their eyes open at about three weeks, at which time they have begun to be marked more clearly with their black masks across their bright black eyes, and with five to seven rings around their handsome tails.

[40]

They purr as they nurse their protective mother, and they sleep in a comfortable warm pile upon the soft, rotted wood within the hollow of the den tree. If one of the raccoon kits gets cold because he is on top of the pile, he crawls under the other little raccoons and is soon warm again.

At about the age of two months they follow their mother down the trunk of the tree, spread-eagle fashion, backing down like bear cubs, clinging for dear life. Often they look fearfully over their shoulders to see how far it is to the forest floor.

They watch their mother closely, and when she digs for earthworms they dig too. When she pulls bark from a fallen log in search of grubs, she has several little helpers. At the edge of the lake or stream they hesitate as their mother wades boldly into the shallows to search with sensitive hands for minnows and crayfish. But when she trills a sharp command, they reply softly in the same language, and soon they are learning the all-important lesson of how to fish.

Who could imagine that in only a year the females of this litter will be leading their own kits down a den tree, along a woodland path and to the water's edge?

IN a secluded spot where the spring foliage will blend with their dappled, tawny coats, the doe has her fawns. The first year she usually has only one. In later springs she often has two.

She is a very good mother, and most of her fawns are good babies. When she tells them to lie right where they are, and please to stay there until she returns, they mostly mind. When a fawn arises from the bed of leaves and flowers and tries to follow his mother, she sometimes pushes him down with her nose and tells him firmly that he is being a wayward fawn. Wait for me, she says; I will soon come back and give you another meal. I can't produce milk unless you let me browse on fresh young leaves and last fall's white-oak acorns. I might even wade for a while in the little lake and dunk for moss and seaweed. Wait right here, beloved.

She moves through sun and shadow like the elusive spirit of spring, down the hillside through the silver beech trees, grazing on grass and flowers. She tips her beautiful ears forward for sounds of danger, watches carefully, sniffing the spring air, always mindful of the fact that she has more than one life to protect: her own and that of the fawns. She steps daintily into the shallows of the little lake, looking this way and that, puts her muzzle into

the clear cold water to drink, nibbles a bit of greenery beneath the surface.

The season of spring is coming along very well. Two nice fawns—handsome twins—no bobcats or bears in these protected woods. The hungry winter is behind her, and she has added two more members to the growing herd she will later lead through the blazing crimson and gold of autumn. She is a happy mother, and the fawns will be waiting where she left them as she climbs the hill again. They will be rewarded as they nurse their wise and wary mother.

SPRING is literally the product of sunlight, a form of gold more precious than the metal. And the earth in turn mirrors this gift of the sun.

If you will cut a few twigs of forsythia in mid-March and put them in a vase of water near a window, you soon will have a blossoming spray of little yellow flowers. In the garden beyond, the forsythia shrubs are soon a mass of gold.

All through April and into May the daffodils bloom. They are mostly yellow cups filled with sunshine, although others may be pink or white. Daffodils have one characteristic very rewarding to the gardener. Mice, moles and chipmunks will not eat the bulb. And the early green leaves are left untouched by the deer. This is not true of the yellow cottage tulips, for tulip bulbs are like candy to many burrowing animals. The leaves make a delicious salad for hungry deer.

In May comes an entire coverlet of gold when the dandelions bloom. Considered a weed by most gardeners and those who like a neat lawn, the dandelions are in fact among our most delicate flowers. If they were as rare as orchids or the night-blooming cereus, people would travel for miles to see a dandelion in bloom. But, like the goldfinch, the "common dandelion" is taken for granted, although it is in truth one more miracle of spring. Its leaves make excellent greens, its flowers a very potable wine, and from its roots come essences used by drug concerns to make tonics. If we had no other source of rubber, we would gather the latex in its sticky sap. How could children do without these sunbursts of yellow brought as gift bouquets to Mother?

Finally there are the winged seeds, the dandelion granddaddies, upon which one must blow once, twice, perhaps three times to tell how many years it will be until one's wish comes true. Off on the wind float the small umbrellas to seed other fields with the light of spring.

The dandelions and yellow tulips, the gold of the flicker and the wild canary, drift on into June when the old-fashioned yellow briar roses conclude the months that have been ablaze with gold ever since the forsythia cuttings gave us promise of another sunlit season.

[46]

THERE are at least forty varieties of wrens and more than one hundred varieties of warblers. The naturalist who says he can identify them all (particularly the warblers in both spring and autumn plumage) is a rare individual indeed.

However, there are not so many varieties of kinglets. Most bird watchers are soon able to tell the ruby-crowned from the golden-crowned kinglet for the simple reason that the one has a ruby crown and the other a golden crown, seldom seen unless the bird is excited or angry.

The smallest bird on our continent is the ruby-throated hummingbird, whose identity is obvious as he hovers iridescently before the chalice of a flower. The golden-crowned kinglet and ruby-crowned kinglet come in only slightly larger packages, being scarcely four inches in length. They are small, lively, olive-gray, rather chunky little birds with sharp beaks. The male ruby-crowned shows the flash of red on his small head in moments of emotion. His wife has no such danger signal. The golden-crowned has a yellow patch; his wife's is somewhat duller.

Only slightly larger than the kinglets are the wrens. The house wren is about five inches in length, nearly an inch longer than the eastern winter wren. The male usually comes north earlier than the female, and builds several nests for any potential mate who might be interested. Nothing like offering a choice of apartments! He sings "Terr-wheedle-wheedle-wheedle, widdle-widdle-widdle" because he is trying to wheedle-wheedle-wheedle some female wren into becoming his wife.

Both male and female wrens are bold little birds, but the female may become something of a tyrant. With so many nests to choose among (and, for that matter, so many males), she sometimes accepts the mate but none of his nests, and will tear a nest apart and build it all over again to her own liking.

It isn't size that matters. It's spunk.

ONE expects criticism when writing a book, but not such violent criticism as I have received from a ruffed grouse while writing this page about the species.

I admire these big, handsome birds with their rich tweed-colored feathers and fan-shaped tail bordered with black. Sometimes they startle me, as I walk our woodland paths, by roaring up from the forest floor with a thunder of wing music that vibrates through the slanting sunlight like the deepest notes of an organ.

It always moves me when a mother grouse, like so many ground-nesting birds, pretends to have a broken

wing as she limps away from her nest to keep us from damaging her eggs or newly hatched chicks. I wish I could talk grouse language and tell her that I would not hurt her eggs or babies for all the broiled grouse in North America.

The crested male had been drumming on his favorite log most of the morning, for it is the season of the year when the proud cock attracts females to his log. Then I heard that wild thunder of the male grouse, coming through the air like a seventeen-inch missile. He hit one of the twenty-six panes of the picture window over my desk. I ducked as the shattering glass sprayed me.

"Gladys dear," I called, "we need the eyedropper and strong coffee. It's another ruffed grouse."

We had saved three grouse, two Kentucky warblers and several ovenbirds by this medicinal method. We have found that if they haven't broken their necks when they hit a window, they can usually be revived with a drop or two of stimulant to bring them out of shock.

It was a large bird. Its neck had not been broken, and it needed about five drops to revive it. Then it shook its beautiful crested head and rose to its feet.

We let it fly from the back porch with its usual roar of wing music. And we can only conjecture what his favorite hen said when he began, "Guess what happened to me as I was trying to miss the Sterling North house."

HE picks the acreage. She chooses the site for the nest. At least, that is often the case with a pair of happily mated birds. Like most pioneer Americans, the male usually leads the way on a migration. But it is the later-arriving female who decides exactly what view she wants from the window.

In the case of the woodpeckers the male may suggest this tree or that, but it is the female who makes the final choice, which is as it should be in home hunting.

Of course, if they have used the nest before and feel that it needs only a little patching and redecorating, with a new lining of fur or feathers or thistledown, much argument is saved. They can spend most of their time courting and then settle down to egg laying and incubation.

Eastern phoebes, those aerial gymnasts and nervous little flutter-tails, have built their nests for seventeen consecutive years in a niche in the stone wall beside the entrance to our lower terrace, making that door unusable for much of the summer. For nesting material they use mud and wet moss from the edge of the waterfall. Not far above them, on a cornice under the eaves, robins regularly make a nest of mud and grass. Like many plasterers, they leave quite a mess to be cleaned up after them.

But the neat little song sparrows among the budding roses, and the friendly catbirds in the barberry bush present no problems and much pleasure; the mourning doves with their makeshift platform of twigs speak softly and with soothing sadness from the hemlock. Within view of the terrace is a hollow silver beech again occupied by wood ducks, an old elm penetrated by pileated woodpeckers, and a wild cherry where a pair of green herons is nesting. A few yards up the trail an ovenbird has built her domed-over bower at the base of a big white oak tree. And on a marshy point, a female mallard has made her nest of reeds lined with down plucked from her own breast.

High on the ridge above our valley, at the top of a tall dead tulip tree, a hawk has refurbished last year's nest, defying the storms. We think that *we* own this valley, but so do some ninety-six varieties of birds, the deer, the foxes and the raccoons. We live in harmony, as neighbors should. They have built their houses and we have built ours. And out of mutual respect the land is protected as a haven that, Fate willing, may save us all.

MOST *passerine* birds (those that perch) lay from 3 to 5 eggs, with a remarkably consistent average of 4. And with few exceptions they have the mysterious ability to control their egg production.

No amateur should ever molest a nest. But the trained scientist who knows what he is doing, and who needs egg samples for a museum, can carefully lift one egg from a nest, prick holes at each end, blow out the contents, seal the little holes, and add it to some nature display without disturbing the mother bird or lessening her hatch. Some birds, put to the test, have laid as many as 67 replacements after single eggs were removed once a day.

Generally speaking, during the egg-laying period most birds can lay an egg a day. So, of course, can domestic hens. And one amazing duck has a record of 363 eggs in 365 days. Production in the wild ranges from 1 egg a year, credited to the extinct great auk and the also extinct passenger pigeon, to clutches of 20 eggs, not unusual for pheasants. Sometimes it seems that the more endangered the bird, the more eggs it lays. A dozen or more eggs are not unusual for the much-hunted wild ducks. For Canada geese, 3 to 7 are usual, with 4 goslings frequently brought to maturity.

In size, the eggs range from a tiny oval pearl, not much larger than a navy bean, laid by the jewel-like hummingbird, to the egg of the extinct elephant birds of Madagascar, which had a two-gallon capacity, six times that of an ostrich egg. But, again, size is of little importance. And who would not cherish that dazzling flash of miniature perfection—a hummingbird poised before a deep-throated flower? Beauty frequently comes in small packages.

MOST of the tree-nesting birds brood their eggs for a period of 10 to 20 days. Our song sparrows usually take 11 or 12 days, and our robins, 13. Our blue jays and crows take 17 or 18 days, and our great black eastern ravens about 3 weeks.

Many of our ground-nesting birds take somewhat longer, but are born much more fully developed. Unlike the typically naked and blind birds of the trees, these groundlings are covered with down, leave the egg with bright eyes wide open, and can run or swim from the nest almost immediately. If the mother quail or grouse or duck sounds a note of warning, these *precocial* birds will scamper from the nest for better cover. Soon they start finding their own food. And although they are usually led by their mother, who also broods them for warmth at night or during a storm, they demand very little parental labor compared to the passerine birds.

These ever-hungry tree nestlings, with yellow, orange or red mouths wide open, keep their parents frantically busy for two or three weeks. It takes a worm a minute to satisfy a baby cardinal. We have counted 792 visits to the nest between dawn and dark by the eastern phoebe at our terrace door. Sometimes both parents are exhausted by the time the young have taken their first flight.

But parental love is another wonder of nature. And the mother bird, sighing with weariness and satisfaction, says to the father bird, "Let's do it again next spring!"

IT is no wonder that the trees of our forest look like the pipes of a cathedral organ. From the first whispered notes of predawn, swelling into the music of dawn itself, the harmonies continue in varying volume all day, with some of the most beautiful melodies coming from the throats of thrushes as the amber light of evening appears.

Bird songs in our valley are at their best in April, May and early June, and then become more hushed for the rest of the summer.

James Russell Lowell was right. What, indeed, *is* so rare as a day in June? The cherry trees so recently white with blossoms are now hung with fruit for birds and children to enjoy. Water lilies float upon our lakes and streams. And millions of fledglings are learning the art of flight.

In our endangered world the promise has again been kept. We have been granted *one more spring!*

List of Illustrations